THE BANSTEAD & EPSOM DOWNS RAILWAY

J. R. W. Kirkby

THE OAKWOOD PRESS
1983

ISBN 085361 300 1

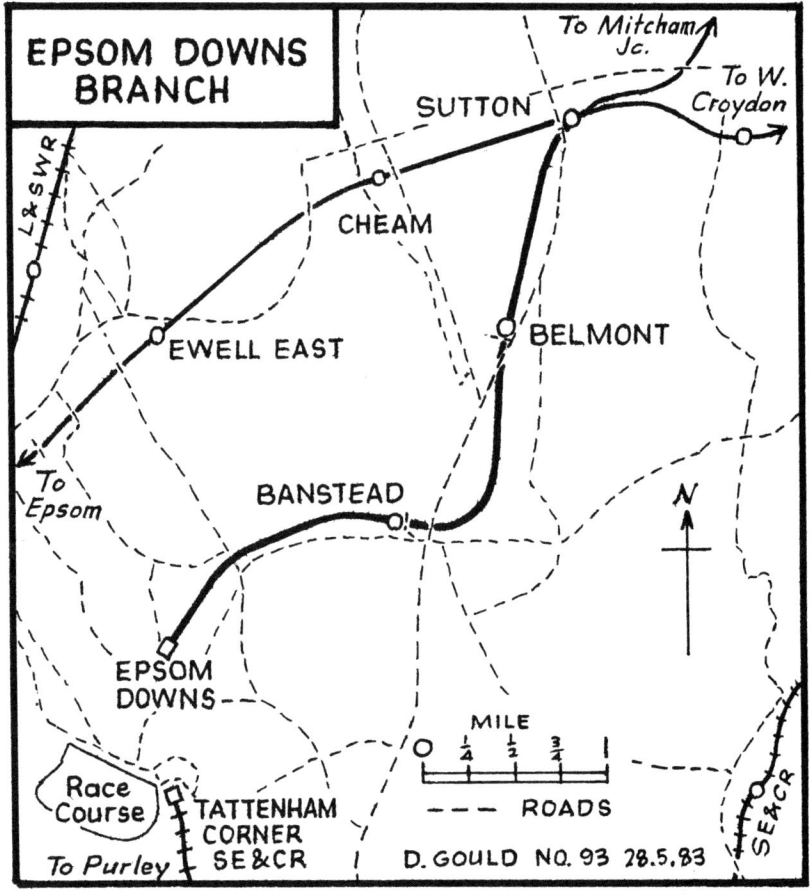

CHAPTER I
Origins

The Banstead & Epsom Downs Railway was born out of horse-racing. Horse-racing, the discovery of Epsom salts and the activities of a strange woman known as "Crazy Sally" put the little town of Epsom on the map in the early seventeenth century. During the hot, dry summer of 1618 a herdsman, looking for water for his cattle, came upon a water hole on the common between Epsom and Ashtead. He was surprised to find his animals would not drink it and on tasting it himself, found it salty. A number of physicians and apothecaries visited the hole and decided that the water had no medicinal properties, so it was not until 1632, when some less squeamish labourers drank copiously from the hole with very uncomfortable results, that the real value of Epsom salts was discovered. From that day the town grew in importance.

Crazy Sally was skilled at bone-setting which brought people from miles around to receive her ministrations—she lived in Epsom about the same time. The exact date on which horse-racing on the downs above Epsom began is not certain but general opinion seems to be that it was around 1630. Samuel Pepys records in his diary on 25th May 1663—"a great throng going to the downs upon a great horse and foot race".

Regular Spring and Summer race meetings were established in 1730 and in 1773 Lord Derby acquired a property in Woodmansterne known as "The Oaks". The first "Oaks" race for three-year-old fillies was run in 1779—the first "Derby" on 4th May 1780.

Epsom races became extremely popular with rich and poor alike, and although there was no public transport of any kind, thousands of people from all over south-east England would converge on Epsom Downs on foot, horseback or any animal-drawn contrivance they could lay their hands on. Even after the arrival of railways local people who remember Derby days in the late nineteenth century describe how the Brighton road south of Sutton would, by noon, become a seething mass of horse-drawn vehicles, the wealthy in their carriages, the poor in their carts, many already full of ale and lashing their unfortunate animals up the hill to the Downs to get to the races on time.

It was some 200 years from the start of racing at Epsom before people could travel there by train. In May 1838 the London and Southampton Railway opened up its line specially between Nine Elms and Woking Common earlier than planned, and arranged for eight trains to set down passengers at a point where their line crossed the Kingston to Epsom Road, near where Surbiton station now stands. 5,000 people descended on Nine Elms; the railway was overwhelmed and many were disappointed. Four years later the London and Brighton Railway made similar arrangements at Stoats Nest, near Coulsdon, which involved a walk of seven miles to the racecourse.

Despite an attempt by the London & South Western Railway to project a branch from Kingston (now Surbiton) to Epsom, it was the London, Brighton & South Coast Railway which first reached Epsom from West Croydon on 10th May 1847, just in time for the Derby of that year. Twelve years later, in 1859, the L.&S.W.R. also reached Epsom from Raynes Park and the value of the race traffic at that time can be judged from the comments of the L.B.&S.C.R. Chairman in that year, who blamed a fall in total receipts of his company on the loss of some race traffic to the L.&S.W.R.

Nevertheless the race traffic continued to grow and with a view to cashing in on this seemingly lucrative business a group of local professional men got together and formed a company known as the Banstead & Epsom Downs Railway Company to build a railway from Sutton to Epsom Downs. They applied to Parliament and received authority (25 and 26 Vict. cap 158) on 17th July 1862.

Following this a meeting of the Company was held in the chambers of Messrs. Gregory and Champion at 18 Clements Inn, London on 24th July 1862 at which the following were present: Ralph Walters, Dr. Pearce Nesbitt, Cooke Baines, George Parker, Alexander Beattie M.D., Thomas Gregory.

At this meeting Walters became Chairman, and Beattie Deputy Chairman. Captain Flower was appointed Engineer and the seal of the Company was approved. Thomas Gregory resigned from the Board to become their legal adviser, little realising then the extent to which his services were going to be required. Four days later a second meeting was held when Raymond Gates was appointed Secretary to the Company. A move by Parker and Nesbitt to have the latter's son appointed to this position was defeated and probably heralded the troubles that were to follow.

Also at this meeting the Solicitor and Engineer were asked to make formal contact with the London, Brighton & South Coast Railway who had already given informal blessing to the project; Chairman, Secretary and Solicitor were called upon to arrange an issue of shares and it was agreed that a Mr. Shrimpton be requested to make a detailed written proposal for the construction of the line. Finally the Rt. Hon. F. Byng was appointed to the Board vice Mr. Gregory.

Then the trouble started. It appears that a Mr. Gurney, who had been instrumental in getting the Bill through Parliament, had made some form of promise or contract with a Mr. Shields for the construction of the Railway and at a meeting of the earlier group had handed a document to this effect to Mr. Champion who did not read it at the time and subsequently did nothing about it. At a meeting of the Company on 7th August it is recorded that the Directors did not sanction Mr. Gurney to enter into any contract with Mr. Shields and approved one of the tenders submitted by Mr. Shrimpton.

On 4th October a meeting was held when it was recorded that "Mr.

Shrimpton having stated to the Board that arrangements are likely to be made for a transfer of his contract to another person the meeting was adjourned and a special meeting called for 11th Oct." At this meeting there was a terrible row, Parker refused to sign the Directors' attendance book or vote for acceptance of the minute of 4th October and resigned. Nesbitt also refused to sign the Directors' attendance book and did not attend another meeting for some time, while in the meantime an agent of the Gurney/Shields contract, called Garratt, started work on the line. Captain Flower, engineer to the Company, said he had not countenanced Garratt starting work on the line and believed his "doings" were the result of clandestine initiatives by Parker and Gurney.

At the first shareholders' meeting on 27th November 1862 Capt. Flower was instructed by the Board to prepare a report giving "such explanation as he can in reference to the unwarrantable interference of a person by the name of Garratt". Capt. Flower failed to make a report, preferring "to abide by the views of persons assuming to be Directors" and was prompty dismissed. A Mr. Bird was appointed Engineer on 23rd January 1863.

This poor little Railway was now really in trouble. Not only was there an official and an unofficial Board of Directors both setting about building the line, but a Bill had been lodged in Chancery: Garratt v Shrimpton and the Banstead & Epsom Downs Rly Co., and writs had been served on the Company by Walters, Parker and Nesbitt. In retaliation these gentlemen had been given notice by Gregory that they would be held responsible for any damage caused by their improperly representing themselves to be the "Company" and that "such proceeding shall be taken against them as shall be advised".

While all these things were happening the Company bravely tried to carry on its normal business, one of the more interesting matters being a proposal to extend the line from Epsom Downs to Dorking; but in January 1863 it was reported that there was no time to get the Bill through in the current session of Parliament and the proposal was abandoned. At about the same time the Company was advised by its Solicitors that notices had been advertised for a new railway bearing the title "London and Epsom Downs Railway" in which the London, Chatham & Dover Railway were involved. The Banstead & Epsom Downs Board promptly asked their Solicitor to petition against the new proposal.

The London & Epsom Downs Railway proposed to build a station only 220 yards from the Grandstand, and at about the same time the Banstead & Epsom Downs Company received an approach from the London, Brighton & South Coast Railway offering a 4% working contract on the share capital provided an additional half mile was built to take the railway to the Grandstand.

In the event both attempts to bring a railway nearer the racecourse were frustrated by the combined opposition of the Racecourse Association and John Briscoe M.P., Lord of the Manor and freeholder of Epsom Downs.

The latter, in the end, sold the plot on which Epsom Downs station now stands some five furlongs from the Grandstand, and it was not to be until 4th June 1901 when the South Eastern Railway opened Tattenham Corner station that people could travel by train to within a few hundred yards of the course.

In March 1863 Mr. Shrimpton reported that he had entered into negotiations with a Party for the disposal of his Contract which would lead to the transfer of the direction and management of the affairs of the Banstead & Epsom Downs Railway into the hands of gentlemen forming part of the London, Brighton and South Coast Railway Company.

Because the Board believed this proposal would put an end to "the vexatious litigation" into which they had been drawn and would relieve them of further trouble and responsibility, they accepted the proposal subject to certain personal financial safeguards and a new Board was constituted under the chairmanship of Mr. Leo Schuster with Mr. Sleight (Secretary to the L.B.&S.C.R.) as Secretary. Shortly afterwards, in June 1864, the Banstead & Epsom Downs Railway Company was amalgamated into the London, Brighton & South Coast Company.

The short, stormy life of the Banstead & Epsom Downs Company illustrates clearly the risks run by amateurs who, in those earlier years, tried to promote small railways here, there and everywhere. Equally it demonstrates how, when a group of people get together to do something, they so often split into factions; enthusiasm overcomes common sense and unless legal ends are securely tied and management is in experienced hands, disaster can be just around the corner. Nevertheless the railway from Sutton to Epsom Downs was opened to traffic on 22nd May 1865 and during Epsom Races that week some 70,000 people were conveyed by it.

CHAPTER II
The Railway

The line was double from the start to accommodate the race traffic. Sutton, in 1865, was a two-platform wayside station midway between Croydon and Epsom. The branch started with a double-track junction east of Sutton station and turned immediately south on a 12-chain curve. The Epsom line platforms (Nos. 1 and 2) were straight while the Branch platforms (Nos. 3 and 4) were sharply curved, the station facilities being mainly in the fork of the two lines or on the Brighton Road which passed over both Epsom and Epsom Downs lines. F. Richards in his book *Sutton, Surrey and its surroundings* says the Railway Company erected new waiting rooms and booking offices in 1865 when the branch was opened for traffic. Crossovers were provided a short way up the branch and at the London end of the branch platforms; the latter were removed in 1925.

Leaving Sutton the line climbs at gradients varying between 1 in 58 and 1 in 66 to the first station which has a somewhat unique history. There are several variations on the tale of how Belmont came to be, but I favour the views of G.H. Kingshott, a local historian. Belmont did not exist in 1865, the land there being part of the parish of Cheam. Kingshott relates how a certain John Gibbons, resident in the area, was charged with poaching for which the punishment at that time was deportation. He decided to beat the system and absconded to America where he eventually joined the California gold rush and became a relatively rich man. His grandmother held the licence for an ale house known as "Little Hell" just off the Brighton Road on the site of the present station. When Gibbons finally returned he built a public house on the other side of the road, transferred his grandmother's licence to it and called it the "California Arms".

He then sold "Little Hell" to the Banstead & Epsom Downs Railway, where the first station was built one mile 8 chains from Sutton. The L.B.&S.C.R., who had by then taken over the line, already having a station at Cheam, called the new station California. Kingshott goes on to relate how, with the coming of the railway, the district began to develop, and because officially there was no such place in England as California, only a railway station and a pub, traffic destined for the area would quite often be exported to America. Poor Mr. Fleetwood, stationmaster at the time, received so many complaints about lost consignments that his wife, fearing for his health, suggested the station be called Belmont, to which the L.B.&S.C.R. agreed and so it became on 1st October 1875. A newer public house called "The California" stands there to this day.

A road from Cheam which joined the Brighton Road near the "California", originally crossed the railway by a level crossing immediately south of the station but in 1888 the existing steeply humped bridge was built and Station Road as it became known was diverted over it. The level crossing was closed but the old road still runs down to the railway on either side.

Mystery surrounds the actual date when the goods yards on the line were opened. Plans exist dated 1865, the year the line opened, showing yards at both California and Banstead but goods trains did not appear in the working timetables until 1872 and only then on a very limited basis.

At California the goods yard was initially between the level crossing and Brighton Road bridge, a very restricted site which necessitated the two sidings being reached by means of a wagon turntable at the end of the Dock siding which had a trailing connection off the Down branch line. When the level crossing was closed and replaced by a bridge, the goods yard was moved to the other side of the Brighton Road and the connection with the branch line was just south of the Brighton Road bridge. At first operated by ground frame, this connection was later worked from the signal box and communication between signalmen and yard staff was by a loud sounding bell on the loading gauge post at the entrance to the yard.

Eventually the station had two trailing crossovers, one at the north end of the station, the other just south of the goods yard connection, between which 40 wagons could be run round. There was also a short refuge siding on the Down side immediately north of the station with a capacity of 17 wagons and for a few years there was a siding behind the Up platform known as Metropolitan Schools siding, removed about 1889.

From California to the next station—Banstead—the railway continued to rise at 1 in 61 to 1 in 70. The line bisected Banstead Downs and after about half a mile entered a deep cutting, turning right to pass first under the Brighton Road for the third and last time and then the Banstead–Ewell road on which Banstead station was built. On the stretch south of California before entering the cutting there was for many years a footpath which crossed the railway by means of stiles. On this stretch also sparks from locomotives tackling the gradient frequently caused gorse and grass fires in dry weather.

Some of the chalk excavated from the cutting was dumped on the common land on either side of the line, and has since become largely overgrown, but these lumps are still known locally as "The Chalk Hills", upon which people take Sunday walks or exercise their dogs. Halfway between California and Banstead a bridge was built carrying a cart track across the railway and to enable farmers to move stock from one side of the railway to the other. This bridge is still known as "The Sheep Bridge" and subsequently became a favourite spot for suicides.

Banstead station is over a mile from Banstead village and, as at California, the goods yard is on the Down side. Eventually here also there were trailing crossovers on either side of the station and in later years there were chalk sidings on the Up side between Ewell Road and Brighton Road Bridges and on the Down side south of the goods yard. From both these large quantities of chalk were loaded away in railway wagons until soon after World War I.

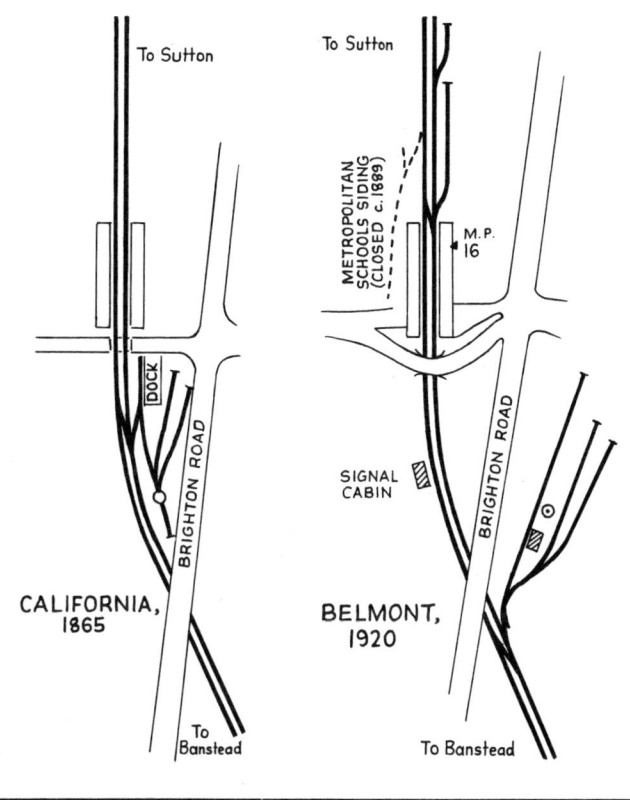
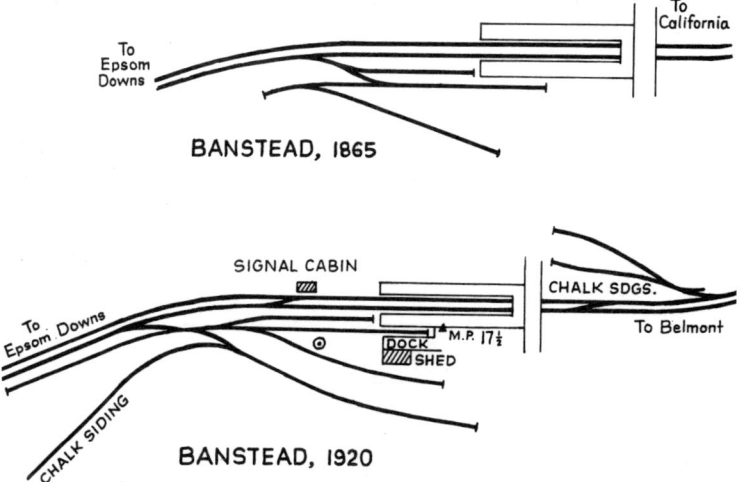

From Banstead the line fell to cross the Ewell–Burgh Heath road at Drift Bridge then rose slightly to the terminus at the foot of Epsom Downs, 4 miles 10 chains from Sutton.

Epsom Downs station, built to accommodate race traffic, consisted of nine platforms with "middle sidings" between platforms 3/4 and 5/6 with crossover roads between the platform lines and middle siding at both ends. There was a 42ft. turntable with coal stage and tank house with water columns at the north end of platforms 3, 4, 5 and 6 and in the Down siding near the signal box. On the Up side there were three carriage sidings and on the Down side two with long shunt sidings on each side. There was no goods yard and the only goods traffic handled was smalls traffic in the platforms, wagons of railway stores, wagons for private sidings and odd public consignments by special arrangement.

The early forms of signalling on the branch are obscure. Until 1874, apart from race days, only one train was on the branch at any one time, but in that year a signal box was installed at California. A signal box was provided at Banstead about 1877 and on 27th May 1879 a new wooden signal box with spindle frame was brought into use at Epsom Downs in time for the races that year. In common with most of the L.B.&S.C.R. the signalling was renewed and modernised around the turn of the century. New wooden signals boxes with brick bases were brought into use at Banstead in 1903 and Belmont in 1909, whilst in 1908 the box at Epsom Downs was relocked with tappets. Both Banstead and Belmont boxes had tappet frames and closing switches and Tyers instruments were in use throughout the branch.

In the very early days there was an instruction in the Appendix to the Working Timetables which read "The line will be closed after the last train every night until 30 minutes before the first train in the morning is due. All signal lights to be put out. The line is closed on Sundays when the passenger service is suspended." After the rebuilding of the signal boxes it became the practice to leave the signal lamps burning all night.

In order to cope with the ever-increasing race traffic three new intermediate signal boxes were built. "B" Intermediate between Belmont and Banstead was opened in 1901 whilst "A" Intermediate between Sutton and Belmont and "C" Intermediate between Banstead and Epsom Downs were opened in 1902. Each had home, starting, advanced starting and distant signals in each direction, but the arms were only put on the posts and worked during race weeks and in Southern Railway days this was confined to Derby week. The arms had no spectacle glasses and no lamps were provided as these boxes were only ever switched on during daylight hours.

Epsom Downs was also provided with an additional outer home signal on these occasions, thus providing 19 stop signals on the Down line and 16 on the Up line over the four miles. The author has stood on Belmont station on a Derby day and seen three Down trains in view at one time.

On the country end of the Up branch platform (No. 3) at Sutton a wooden shunting cabin was erected in 1878 which could control the crossover, four shunt signals and a starting signal to allow a train for the branch to depart from the Up branch platform. This cabin was strictly speaking a ground frame and was opened when required, but during the era of rail motor operation it was open for most of the time passenger services were running.

The principal changes in the infrastructure over the years have been:

1880	Crocketts Siding installed about ¼ mile beyond Banstead on the Down line to serve Kensington and Chelsea District Schools. This siding was operated by Annett's key kept in Banstead signal box.
1886	Gadesden's Siding installed about ¼ mile from Epsom Downs on the Up line to serve North Looe Farm. This siding was operated by Annett's key kept in Epsom Downs signal box.
1/6/1898	Banstead station renamed Banstead and Burgh Heath.
6/1922	Repeater starting and shunt signals at the country end of platform 3 at Sutton repeating those at the country end of platform 4, removed.
1/4/1925	A.C. electric trains commenced working to Sutton. Overhead wires extended up the Epsom Downs branch to a point one train's length beyond the trailing crossover south of Sutton.
17/6/1928	D.C. Third rail electrification completed to Epsom Downs including six platforms at that terminus. Down line platforms at Belmont and Banstead extended to accommodate 8-car electric trains. Refuge siding and north crossover at Belmont removed.
8/1928	Banstead and Burgh Heath station renamed Banstead.
2/1931	Locomotive turntable at Epsom Downs removed.
11/10/1940	Belmont station house and Down side buildings destroyed by enemy action. Temporary wooden booking office subsequently installed on Up side. Up side platforms at Belmont and Banstead extended to take 8-car trains.
11/1955	"A", "B" and "C" Intermediate signal boxes removed. Last used 8/1955.
12/1956	L.B.&S.C.R. Inner Home signals at ends of Epsom Downs platforms removed and replaced by Platform Indicator attached to Outer Home signal.
7/9/1964	Banstead Goods Yard closed.
1/8/1965	Belmont Crossover removed.
6/1/1969	Belmont Goods Yard closed. It handled coal only from 3/1/1966.
30/7/1969	Sutton Ground Frame abolished.
7/12/1969	Banstead Crossovers removed.

21/12/1969	Belmont and Banstead signal boxes abolished. Track Circuit Block introduced between Sutton and Epsom Downs boxes.
5/1970	Belmont station finally rebuilt on the Down side.
4/6/1972	Platforms 1, 2, 3, 6 and 7 put out of use at Epsom Downs. Platforms 5 and 6 renumbered 1 and 2.
16/11/1981	Epsom Downs signal box destroyed by fire. Single line working introduced using the Up line.
4/10/1982	Double track restored between Sutton station and a point some 40 yards on the Belmont side of Ventnor Road bridge midway between Sutton and Belmont. From that point the line is single to Epsom Downs over the old Down line and the Up line has been recovered. The signalling is now controlled from the new electronic signal box at Victoria.

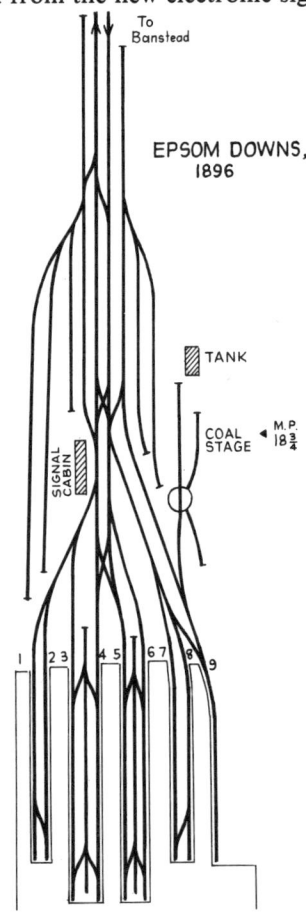

EPSOM DOWNS, 1896

CHAPTER III
Management and Working Arrangements

In the early days of railways the management structure provided for a stationmaster at almost every station with Traffic, Permanent Way, Signalling and other Inspectors located at important centres all reporting direct to one headquarters. As the size of railways and the traffic density grew the day-to-day task of running the railway became too big to be performed effectively from one location so this function was delegated to District or Divisional Officers.

The London, Brighton & South Coast Railway was no exception and in its later years there were District Superintendents (Operating), District Engineers and District Goods Managers at East Croydon and Brighton. The Epsom Downs branch came under East Croydon, although before World War I there was for a time a small district presence at Sutton.

Following amalgamation in 1923 the Southern Railway divided its system into six districts and the Epsom Downs branch came under the London East Division based on London Bridge, which included parts of the former L.B.&S.C.R. and S.E.C.R. suburban systems. This lasted until 1930 when the operating and commercial departments were combined and five Divisions replaced the six Districts and the Epsom Downs branch became part of the London Central Division which comprised most of the former L.B.&S.C.R. The headquarters was first at London Bridge, moved to Redhill on the outbreak of World War II and finally to East Croydon where, after a number of changes to title and degree of delegation of authority, it has remained ever since.

On the Civil Engineering side the branch, after amalgamation, came under the Southern District Engineer at East Croydon until that office was closed in 1933 and responsibility was transferred to the London East Division Engineer at London Bridge who later moved to the old engine shed at Purley and finally to Southern House at East Croydon. In L.B.&S.C.R. and S.R. days there was a Carriage and Wagon Department office at Sutton and for signalling purposes there was a mechanical lineman at Sutton and an electrical lineman at West Croydon.

In the event of accident or derailment the nearest breakdown crane was at New Cross (later Bricklayers Arms) and the nearest Tool Van at Battersea (Norwood from 1935). In steam days there were four single ramps kept in the Tank house at Sutton and Hand and Traverser Jacks in the Lamp Room and Carriage and Wagon lobby at Sutton.

All through the life of the L.B.&S.C.R. the three stations on the branch each had its own stationmaster and it was not until 1927 when Mr. Scholbert of Epsom Downs died and Mr. Sawyer of Belmont was promoted to Dulwich, that Mr. Reynolds of Banstead took charge of all three, an arrangement which lasted until August 1966 when the post was redesignated Station Manager. A year later, on 31/7/1967, it was relocated to Epsom Downs and finally abolished on 25/3/73 when the branch came under the station manager at Sutton.

Steam passenger rolling stock in daily use was at times berthed overnight at Epsom Downs and for a short period in 1925 at Banstead. After electrification of the branch a motorman's signing-on point was set up at Epsom Downs under a foreman motorman, and electric stock was berthed in the platforms there overnight and during the off-peak. In 1938, for instance, six 8-car trains were berthed overnight and seven three-car sets and six 2-car trailers berthed between the morning and evening peaks on Mondays to Fridays. This involved the employment of carriage cleaning staff at Epsom Downs.

Difficulty in getting staff in the area and the need for economy and tighter management finally decided B.R. to concentrate most of its electric rolling stock on the main depots and close the periphery ones. The motorman's signing on point at Epsom Downs was closed on 5/5/69 and the berthing of stock there ceased on 1/5/1972.

Goods wagons were controlled and distributed from the sub-district office at Sutton until the last war when the work was moved to Norwood Yard. All spare wagons in L.B.&S.C.R. days were ordered to Norwood unless required elsewhere.

Various problems in operating passenger and freight services on the branch are dealt with in subsequent chapters, but it is interesting to note that during foggy weather signals on the branch were not provided with fogmen in L.B.&S.C.R. days except for Sutton Junction Up Branch Home with splitting distants on the same post. These signals were inner distants; stop and distant signals on the same post worked from the same box were generally frowned upon and therefore rare. These were believed to be the last examples to survive on the Southern Railway.

After electrification fog signalmen were provided, when possible, at most of the distant signals on the branch.

CHAPTER IV
Passenger Traffic and Services

Apart from race traffic dealt with in another chapter, passenger traffic in the early years was extremely light, although with the advent of the railway there was some building particularly around Belmont station. Banstead Downs, which lie between Belmont and Banstead, were surprisingly included in a conservation scheme which received the Royal assent as long ago as 1893. It was later included in the Surrey County Council Act of 1931 and the London County Council Green Belt Act of 1938. Nevertheless, outside the prescribed areas there was, after the turn of the century, very considerable housing development along the line particularly between the wars and electrification in 1928 gave it further impetus. The number of passengers using the branch annually in 1927 (329,778), had by 1935 increased to 859,794, most of which were commuters to London or off-peak travellers to Sutton, Croydon and London.

Both Banstead and Epsom Downs were popular with weekend ramblers and picnickers and also for school outings and Sunday school treats particularly from those parts of London where the people could not afford fares to the seaside.

The other main feature of the line was the number of hospitals and institutions it served. Belmont hospital was opened as an orphanage in 1852 and during its time became a workhouse, a prisoner of war camp, a home for the destitute and a hospital for nervous disorders. Banstead Mental Asylum on Banstead Downs opened in 1877 and had by 1910 a population of 2,661 inmates and staff. Cuddington Fever Hospital and Kensington and Chelsea District Schools were close by Banstead station while Epsom College was not too far from Epsom Downs station.

The passenger train service can best be described in four phases:
 i Steam train working from 1865 to 1909
 ii Steam Rail Motor working, 1909–1928
 iii D.C. Electric train working, 1928–1967
 iv D.C. Electric train working, 1967–today

I. 1865–1909

The initial service of 1865 comprised 8 trips each way on weekdays and four each way on Sundays worked by a branch engine based on West Croydon and stock based at Sutton. 15 minutes was allowed for the journey but a year later the Up journey was cut to 13 mins. This service proved extravagant and in 1867 was cut back to 3 Down and 4 Up on weekdays and 2 each way on Sundays. On 1st October 1868 the line from Peckham Rye to Sutton was opened and Sutton became an important junction on the new main line to Portsmouth although it was several years before the Portsmouth expresses called at Sutton, the joining and splitting of Victoria and London Bridge portions being performed at Mitcham

Junction. From this date the Sunday service was withdrawn, not to be restored for 36 years, but the weekday service became 7 trains each way daily. The branch train was based at Epsom Downs and started thence at 9.0 am finishing there at 7.13 pm. The locomotive worked a goods trip from Sutton at 7.30 am, and returned similarly from Epsom Downs at 7.45 pm.

The interesting feature was that only a few of the trips were worked by the branch train. Trains to Epsom, Dorking or beyond were worked from London Bridge via either Mitcham Junction or West Croydon and at Sutton made connection with another train by the opposite route, supplemented at times by a train from Victoria via one route or the other as well. A number of these trains filled in their waiting time at Sutton by running to Epsom Downs and back thus bringing locomotives from other suburban depots on to the branch and providing useful route knowledge for race days. Stroudley D1 class tanks monopolised these workings in the late nineteenth century.

This pattern of service lasted until full rail motor working was introduced in 1909, but the number of trains gradually increased until by April 1902 there were 14 each way Monday to Friday and 15 on Saturdays. A few of the trains began to be shown as through services in the working timetables. The 11.49 am Sutton to Epsom Downs was shown to start from London Bridge at 10.55 am from January 1884 and the 1.55 pm similarly from London Bridge at 1.6 pm from January 1891.

In January 1887 a new service was introduced at 8.0 am from Victoria to Sutton via Mitcham Junction whence it ran empty to Epsom Downs and formed a 9.7 am Epsom Downs to Victoria. Apart from a break of about two months this morning service to Victoria continued until electrification in 1928. The Down service became a passenger train throughout to Epsom Downs from September 1894, but after World War I ceased to call at Belmont becoming the only steam train in the timetabled service not to call at one of the intermediate stations, apart from an 8.20 am (Not Saturdays) London Bridge to Banstead which ran for a short time in 1925 and did not call at Belmont.

There was no comparable return train although from June 1897 the front part of the 6.12 pm London Bridge to Sutton via West Croydon was projected through to Epsom Downs.

In April 1903 the 1.6 pm London Bridge to Epsom Downs became a Saturdays Only service, and was put back to 1.27 pm running fast to Norwood Junction—another of the through trains which lasted until electrification.

The last train from Sutton to Epsom Downs was around 7.30 pm until 1898 when in June of that year an 8.15 pm was put on running daily in Summer and Saturdays Only in Winter. From October 1904 it terminated at Banstead, starting back from there at 8.45 pm and became the first service to be booked to terminate intermediately on the branch. A year later two new morning trips and three evening trips turned round at

D1 class 0-4-2T No. 285 "Holmwood" with a train of Stroudley four-wheelers south of Belmont just before the turn of the century (Author's collection)

A view of Epsom Downs station about 1900 (Author's collection)

The entrance to Belmont station from the Brighton Road (Author's collection)

Sutton station not long after the opening of the branch (Author's collection)

The Royal Train headed by I2 class No. 15 south of Belmont on its way to the "Derby" of 1908 (Author's collection)

I3 class No. 23 at Epsom Downs with an Up Pullman Race Special in 1910 (Author's collection)

E5 class 0-6-2T No. 2404 piloting ex-S.E.C.R. H class 0-4-4T No. 1548 on a Pullman Race Special on Derby Day, June 1928 (Dr. I.C. Allen)

An ex-L.C.D.R. R class 0-4-4T, SR No. A658 from Epsom shed, struggling up from Belmont to Banstead with a Race Special from London Bridge on Derby Day, June 1928; mixed 6-wheel and bogie stock (Dr. I.C. Allen)

E4 class No. B563 arrives at Epsom Downs with the daily goods in December 1930 (Dr. I.C. Allen)

E4 class No. 2470 approaching Belmont with the morning goods from Norwood in 1939 (Author)

The view from Station Road bridge at Belmont looking south; "Terrier" No. 662 (Author's collection)

Belmont station in 1920: D1 0-4-2T with 2-car motor set (Author's collection)

"Terrier" No. 661 with the 1905/7 type of Balloon trailer at Belmont; note "Last Vehicle" plate showing train is propelling (Author's collection)

I3 class 4-4-2T on a typically wet Derby Day crosses Banstead Downs with Lord Derby's special train formed from ex-S.E.C.R. Continental stock (Dr. I.C. Allen)

D1 No. B269 entering Sutton with a train from Epsom Downs on 24th May 1926; original Balloon coach at rear (H.C. Casserley)

D1 No. 612 waits at No. 5 platform at Epsom Downs with empty stock for New Cross Gate off one of the mid-day Saturday through trains from London Bridge on 18th December 1926 (H.C. Casserley)

The last regular steam train to leave Epsom Downs, the 7.20 pm to Sutton on Saturday 17th June 1928 (J. Reynolds, Stationmaster)

Two I3 class engines, Nos. 2086 and 2029, double-head a return Pullman Race Special from Epsom Downs approaching Banstead in 1928 (Dr I.C. Allen)

I3 class No. 2076 crosses from the Down main to Branch with a first-class special to Epsom Downs on Derby Day, 1939 (Author)

I3 No. 2091 passes Belmont en route for Epsom Downs with a Pullman Race Special for the Spring Meeting, 18th April 1939. Site of original goods yard at right (Author)

I3 No. 2085 approaches Sutton with a first-class Race Special from Victoria via West Croydon on 1st June 1938. Note standby engine in yard (D.H. Wakely)

I3 No. 2024 and H class No. 1517 passing Belmont Intermediate Down home and Up starter on Belmont Up distant post in 1928 (Dr. I.C. Allen)

I3 No. 2029 crossing Banstead Downs with a first-class Race Special on Derby Day, 1928 (Dr. I.C. Allen)

A Victoria–Epsom Downs electric train approaching Epsom Downs for the Spring Meeting, April 1938; 3-car set made from former L.B.S.C. steam stock (Author)

Banstead and the last train for Epsom Downs left Sutton at 6.55 pm.

In 1904 a Sunday service was restored comprising six trains each way operating only from May to October inclusive.

The winds of change were blowing, however, and the L.B.&S.C.R. was looking for ways of competing with the challenge of trams and omnibuses and reducing operating costs and decided to go for rail motor working on a fairly large scale. From 11th June 1906 A1 Terrier tanks fitted for railmotor working with one "Balloon" trailer began operating seven services each way weekdays and Sundays between West Croydon and Belmont in addition to the normal service.

1909–1928

From October 1909 the branch went over to full rail-motor working. Two rail motors were involved, one based on West Croydon, the other on Sutton for which Epsom shed provided the locomotive. The number of branch trips was increased to 37 each way daily and although the last train to Epsom Downs was still at 7.1 pm, a service to Banstead continued until 10.5 pm with late trains on Wednesdays and Saturdays at 10.30 pm and 12.15 am. The 37 trips were shared as follows:

	To Belmont	*To Banstead*	*To Epsom Downs*
West Croydon Rail Motor	8	8	—
Sutton Rail Motor	2	10*	11
Total:	10	16*	11

*=2 more on Wednesdays & Saturdays.

The West Croydon motor also ran a trip from Banstead to Mitcham Junction (later extended to Wimbledon) while a third rail motor, also based on West Croydon, worked a 2.55 pm (Not Saturdays) Victoria to Banstead (fast to Mitcham Junction) returning to West Croydon. The use of rail motors into both London termini was a feature of off peak working on the L.B.&S.C.R. at that time.

One casualty of the new service was the morning through train from Epsom Downs to Victoria, but there was such a rumpus that it was restored within a few weeks. The long-established 1.27 pm SO London Bridge to Epsom Downs continued to run, returning at 2.25 pm to Crystal Palace and was joined by a new train at 1.6 pm SO from London Bridge which ran to Banstead via Mitcham Junction returning to Victoria via West Croydon. In October 1911 these were joined by a third Saturday through train at 2.20 pm from Victoria which was formed of main line Portsmouth stock and returned empty to Victoria.

On Sundays 11 branch trips were operated by a West Croydon rail motor, but from June to September each year until World War I these were augmented by the branch motor and seven trips were run to Epsom Downs. The volume of Sunday visitors to the various hospitals etc. grew beyond the capacity of even 4-car rail motors—two vehicles either side of the locomotive—so that from October 1910 a 3.42 pm London Bridge to Banstead via West Croydon was introduced returning at 4.50 pm and in October 1912 a 2.5 pm Victoria to Banstead via West Croydon returning via the same route at 3.55 pm, which at that time was worked by a Tunbridge Wells locomotive between working the 11.48 am Tunbridge Wells to Victoria and 7.10 pm return.

By June 1914 the daily service had grown to 41 trips daily, and both motor-fitted "Terriers" and D1 tanks were in use, the latter usually with two trailers.

At first the Great War made little impact on the Epsom Downs branch service except that Sunday services to Epsom Downs were discontinued, not to be restored until 1928. In fact a 42nd trip (to Belmont) was put on in October 1914 and it was not until January 1916 that the first cuts came—the later two of the three Wednesday and Saturday late trains then running. In January 1917, however, the West Croydon motor did not start out until 9.45 am and three of the five branch trips before 9.0 am were axed as was the 3.0 pm Victoria to Banstead and 5.32 pm Wimbledon to Banstead and back.

Loss of the early-morning trains produced a host of complaints, and as a result one of them was restored by bringing the Epsom engine out earlier. In May 1918 the last of the late trains (10.30 pm) to Banstead on Wednesdays and Saturdays was withdrawn, but was restored in May 1920.

Also in May 1920 an unusual train was introduced leaving Epsom Downs at 12.58 pm (Not Saturdays) for Sutton where it stayed until forming the 2.10 pm Sutton to Victoria via West Croydon. This train worked down empty from New Cross and was formed of Set 73 consisting of a bogie composite and a bogie lavatory composite formed between two bogie third brakes and strengthened by an additional bogie composite and a brake van. This formation was based on Lewes, and worked the 8.8 am to London Bridge via Sheffield Park returning there with the 5.5 pm from Victoria via the same route. From October 1923 the 12.58 pm from Epsom Downs was withdrawn, but the stock came down to Sutton for the 2.10 pm.

At this time the L.B.&S.C.R. was desperately trying to restore its pre-war level of service against a background of shortages of materials and arrears of maintenance, so from February 1921 the early-morning trains on the Epsom Downs branch were restored using a rail motor based on Coulsdon. Between 5.30 am and 9.40 am some 13 suburban trains left Coulsdon for London, so there was less need at that time for rail-motor services between Coulsdon and Crystal Palace. The Coulsdon motor started out at 6.55 am for Crystal Palace, worked 7.38 am Crystal Palace to Banstead, worked three more branch trips each way before returning to Coulsdon via Crystal Palace. From this date also working of the Sutton branch rail motor was transferred from Epsom to West Croydon shed.

By the time of the amalgamation in 1923 the number of branch trips was 46 each way, increased to 47 in July and 49 in October 1923. The morning workings were extremely slick and some of the turnrounds at Sutton were allowed no more than two minutes. Five different West Croydon/Coulsdon rail motors visited the branch daily.

The next major change was the introduction from 1st April 1925 of A.C. electric services between Victoria and Sutton via West Croydon, a prerequisite of which was the relaying of the junction at Sutton so that a train could leave the Up branch platform for the West Croydon line without conflicting with the main line.

The effect on the branch train service was to make it much more self-contained. All the trips to Wallington, West Croydon or Crystal Palace were withdrawn except two to and from West Croydon, although the number of trips to Wimbledon via Hackbridge was increased to five. The Coulsdon motor no longer appeared and although the number of branch trips went to an all-time high of 51 these were all worked by the Sutton branch motor supplemented by one West Croydon motor. One further change was that the 7.45 am Victoria to Epsom Downs was diverted to Cheam and the through Up service at 9.10 am was formed of stock berthed overnight at Banstead off the 8.20 pm ex-London Bridge (Mondays to Fridays) and at Epsom Downs over the weekend off the 1.25 pm SO from London Bridge.

From October 1923 the 4.38 pm London Bridge to Sutton via West Croydon had been extended through to Epsom Downs returning empty to Hackbridge, but from April 1925 this was discontinued and on Mondays to Fridays carriages for Epsom Downs were attached to the rear of the 4.44 pm London Bridge to Uckfield and detached at Norwood Junction whence they departed at 5.0 pm.

Although traffic on the branch continued to grow, the economy of the country was becoming depressed and railways were making economies. From September 1925 eight branch trips were withdrawn, including the 6.16 pm Sutton to Belmont which became the last passenger train booked to turn round at that station. From February 1926 a new early-morning trip appeared at 6.53 am and for the first time the branch opened before 7.0 am but three more later trips were withdrawn, then during most of the General Strike of 1926 the branch was closed completely.

From then until electrification in 1928 only minor changes took place.

1928–1967

D.C. electric trains began to operate between London Bridge, West Croydon and Epsom Downs from Sunday 17th June 1928. Trains ran at 20-minute intervals from 6.0 am until 10.0 am SX, 2.30 pm SO and from 4.0 pm to 7.30 pm SX. At other times trains ran at 30-minute intervals, including Sundays. Departure times were:

		Past each hour	
Peak Hours	From London Bridge	02, 22, 42	Fast between London Bridge
	From Epsom Downs	04, 24, 44	and Norwood Junction*
Off Peak	From London Bridge	02, 32	All stations except Brockley
	From Epsom Downs	00, 30	and Honor Oak Park.
Sundays	From London Bridge	28, 58	All stations
	From Epsom Downs	08, 38	

*One or two Up services called additionally at New X Gate.

These trains were formed of one 2-car trailer set between two 3-car sets during the peaks and at other busy times, and of one 3-car set at other times. When fog working was in operation 8-car trains operated all day.

The headcode for these services was Ȯ

A motorman's signing-on point was set up at Epsom Downs; drivers and firemen who had worked the steam services had some prior claim to the new jobs and until they could move their homes to the area staff trains were run from Selhurst to Epsom Downs at 5.12 am each morning and a similar staff train returned at 12.50 am each night.

During 1929 the Victoria–Sutton A.C. service was gradually converted to D.C. operation and from 6th July 1930 it, too, was projected to and from Epsom Downs. The pattern was similar to the London Bridge trains except that the first four Up trains continued to start from Sutton, the stock coming from Wallington (2), West Croydon and Victoria. The last Down train, 12.08 am from Victoria, terminated at Sutton and returned empty to West Croydon.

The timing of Victoria services was:

		Past each hour	
Peak Hours	From Victoria	18, 38, 58	All stations except
	From Epsom Downs	09, 29, 49	Battersea Park and
			Wandsworth Common
Off Peak	From Victoria	08, 38	As above
	From Epsom Downs	19, 49	
Sundays	From Victoria	18, 48	All stations except
	From Epsom Downs	25, 55	Battersea Park

The headcode for these services was Ṡ, but trains terminating at Sutton did not carry the dot.

During the peak the Victoria trains followed 5 minutes behind those from London Bridge in both directions between Gloucester Road Junction and Epsom Downs. Each service had but a 5-minute turnround at Epsom Downs so the working was fairly tight, but generally reliability proved excellent. Whenever trains were disrupted by weather or mishap it was the usual practice to turn some of the Victoria services back at Sutton or sometimes the Belmont and Banstead stops would be omitted.

During the off-peak most of the Down Victoria services were booked three minutes at Sutton. This not only enabled Belmont and Banstead signal boxes to be switched out but in most cases afforded a connection at Sutton with the Victoria to Epsom via Mitcham Junction service.

The "Staff" trains were discontinued from July 1932.

The pattern of service introduced in July 1930 lasted for 37 years. There were, however, some additions and alterations, the more important being:

23rd July 1932
1.13 pm SO London Bridge to Wallington extended to Epsom Downs returning at 3.12 pm to Wallington. This service was again cut back to Wallington in May 1942 but restored as an Epsom Downs service in October 1946 but only lasted one year and was withdrawn completely in June 1947.

8th July 1934
The leading 3-car set of the 6.49 am Epsom Downs to Victoria was used to work a new 5.15 am to Victoria via Mitcham Junction returning at 6.0 am via the same route to rejoin the rest of its train. This service, which carried headcode O, was, since electrification, the only regular passenger service to use the Epsom Downs Branch to Mitcham Junction line crossover at Sutton Junction and was primarily put on for news, fish and milk traffic previously conveyed on a van train.

On Summer Saturdays, delays resulting from the heavy holiday traffic played havoc with the 5-minute turnrounds at Epsom Downs, so a turnover train was provided leaving Selhurst at 7.22 am and returning from Epsom Downs to London Bridge as an additional passenger train at 12.15 pm in time for the Saturday peak. It called at all stations to Sydenham. It was withdrawn on the outbreak of war and never restored.

6th July 1936
Brockley and Honor Oak Park stations were served by the two "Roundabout" services from London Bridge. In the off peak the Up services were only 3½ minutes apart, leaving a 26½ minute gap every half hour. From this date the S.R. was finally persuaded to stop the Up Epsom Downs–London Bridge trains to plug the gap.

Another gap was filled from 3rd July 1939 when stops at Forest Hill and Sydenham were inserted in the 11.22 am SO London Bridge to Epsom Downs.

5th July 1937
Growth of commuter traffic had already demanded an additional SO train from London Bridge to Epson Downs. Similar demands for a Monday to Friday service were met by diverting the 6.12 pm London Bridge to Holborn Viaduct via West Croydon and St. Helier to Epsom Downs, returning to West Croydon at 8.10 pm.

On the outbreak of World War II a very limited emergency service of one train per hour off peak and two per hour during the peak operated from 11th September 1939, but proved quite inadequate and normal weekday services were restored a week later.

A revised service was introduced on 16th October 1939 which

maintained all early morning and peak services but curtailed off-peak services by 50%, and the last trains from both Victoria and London Bridge were withdrawn, never to be restored. Sunday services were reduced to two per hour on each route and curtailed after 11.0 pm.

From May 1942 there was an even greater cut-back on evening services, the last train for Epsom downs leaving London Bridge at 9.32 pm with trains from Victoria at 9.38, 10.38 and 11.38 pm. In the Up direction the last train left Epsom Downs at 9.30 pm for London Bridge except on Saturdays when there was a 10.49 pm to Victoria, an arrangement which lasted until May 1944 when the 10.49 pm became a daily train.

From October 1946 the full off-peak service was restored except for some late trains. Apart from those mentioned the 11.0 and 11.30 pm from Epsom Downs to London Bridge were not restored while the 10.2 pm from London Bridge terminated at Sutton and the 11.32 pm at West Croydon.

From June 1958, as a result of introduction of the 5-day week, the Saturday services were reduced to two trains per hour on each route all day. The only concession to the few remaining commuters was that the 8.0 and 8.30 am from Epsom Downs to London Bridge ran fast from Norwood Junction and there was an additional train at 8.13 am which lasted two years. In the Down direction and 12.2, 12.32 and 1.2 pm from London Bridge ran fast to Sydenham then Norwood Junction, otherwise the normal off-peak pattern was observed.

By now the effect of fast-growing car ownership was having a serious effect on both peak and off-peak travel particularly in the wealthier southern and south-eastern counties. London suburban services were being heavily subsidised and governments were putting pressure on the railways for greater economies. From June 1961 there was a cut-back on peak services before 7.0 am and after 7.0 pm and from 11th September 1962 most of the off-peak trains between London Bridge and Epsom Downs terminated at Sutton on both weekdays and Sundays. By now it had become obvious that the intricate pattern of electric train services introduced in the late 1920's and early 1930's was not appropriate to the needs of the 1960's and a major review was put in hand, including an extensive market survey.

All this took a long time and on the Central Division of the Southern was not introduced until July 1967.

In the meantime, since the war, the original stock had been reformed into 4-car formations and there had been a gradual replacement by new 4-car sets for most suburban trains. Two-car sets were in use or built for other parts of the system and from time to time wandered on to the Epsom Downs branch, usually in pairs replacing a 4-car set.

The newer sets and the older NOL sets used numerical headcodes and those for the Epsom Downs branch were:

London Bridge and Epsom Downs via West Croydon — 39

Victoria and Epsom Downs via West Croydon — 84
Victoria and Epsom Downs via Mitcham Junction — 0

1967–Today

The July 1967 timetable not only made fundamental changes to the routing of trains but saw the beginning of the departure from the rigid standard interval timetables of the earlier years.

On the London Bridge route the original pattern was broadly retained between 7.0 am and 9.0 am and between 4.0 pm and 7.0 pm and one or two early-morning trains also kept to the West Croydon route, but outside those times and all day Saturday and Sunday the services were diverted via Mitcham Junction. On weekdays trains called at Peckham Rye, Tulse Hill and all stations thence, while on Sundays they called at all stations. The headcode for these trains was 9.

On the Victoria service trains ran at irregular times via Selhurst during peak hours Monday to Friday and at other times terminated at Sutton. An interesting feature was that at the height of the peaks three Up morning and two Down evening services ran fast between Selhurst and Balham producing another headcode—70: Victoria to Epsom Downs semi-fast. This idea was not a success and all the missing stops had been restored by May 1970. There was also one odd service from Victoria to Epsom Downs at 9.18 am SX which ran via Crystal Palace and a 5.51 pm Epsom Downs to Victoria which ran fast from Epsom Downs to Sutton, being only the third train since 1865 booked to omit stations on the branch. From May 1970, the faster peak-hour services between London Bridge and Epsom Downs on Mondays to Fridays called additionally at Forest Hill.

In May 1969 Sunday services ceased.

May 1973 saw yet another upheaval when during the off peak and on Saturdays the Victoria services were extended to Epsom Downs and the London Bridge via Mitcham Junction service terminated at Sutton.

Further peak-hour cuts were made in 1977, then in May 1979 the Victoria service was reduced to a 30-minute interval all day while the London Bridge service via West Croydon was reduced to 11 Down and 10 Up trains Monday to Fridays.

Following the fire in Epsom Downs' signal box on the night of 16th November 1981, one train maintained a roughly half-hourly shuttle service between Sutton and Epsom Downs until introduction of a Victoria–Epsom Downs service on 4th October 1982.

CHAPTER V
Goods and Parcels Services

Goods train services on the Epsom Downs branch first appeared in the working timetables dated 1872 when, as described in Chapter IV, the passenger engine started its day with a goods trip 7.30 am from Sutton and finished with another goods trip 7.45 pm Epsom Downs to Sutton. The journey time was 35 minutes and 10 minutes was allowed at each of the intermediate stations.

In 1873 building materials began to arrive in large quantities for Banstead Asylum opened in 1874. Most of this was handled at California and an additional goods train left Sutton at 10.55 am returning at 11.20 am. Three years later it was extended to Banstead and back and at the same time 7.30 am from Sutton was put back 30 minutes and allowed extra time at both California and Banstead stations. In January 1878 the 10.55 am from Sutton was replaced by an 8.40 am from Norwood which went through to Epsom Downs calling at Sutton, Belmont and Banstead, returning from Epsom Downs at 11.20 am making the same stops. The morning service from Sutton at 7.0 am lasted until February 1917 although the return evening service from Epsom Downs ceased in October 1905.

By May 1882 traffic had grown to the point where a third train was necessary and this left Sutton at 8.0 am, initially only to Belmont but in September of that year it was extended to Banstead.

The working timetables at that time carried a note that "Two or three trucks of potatoes may be conveyed by the 7.35 pm passenger train from Banstead to Epsom Downs to be sent to Sutton by the 7.30 pm which was a passenger train in Summer and a goods train in Winter." These appear to be the only recorded instances of mixed train working on the branch.

From 1880 the Norwood goods served Crockett's siding when required, and from 1886 Gadesden's sidings also. On each occasion the stationmaster concerned had to arrange for a porter to accompany the train and to return to base with the Annett's key when shunting was completed.

From April 1887 the 8.0 am from Sutton was withdrawn, by which time the daily goods from Norwood to Epsom Downs and back was in the hands of one of Mr. Stroudley's E1 class 0-6-0T based at New Cross. The Norwood–Epsom Downs goods remained a New Cross working until 1928 from when it was worked by West Croydon shed until the opening of Norwood in 1935.

Goods traffic continued to be heavy and in April 1908 an instruction was put out that should the loaded traffic for Banstead and Epsom Downs plus the loaded and empty traffic from Belmont exceed the permitted maximum of 22 wagons (including brake van), then the train proceeded to Banstead without the latter and was allowed sufficient time to return to Belmont for the outward wagons. From October 1912 this became a booked arrangement, the train returning engine and brake from Banstead to Belmont at 12.15 pm leaving Belmont again at 1.25 pm.

From July 1907 until December 1909 a conditional timing was published leaving Epsom Downs at 7.25 pm and was required to run whenever the regular train was overloaded—i.e. more than 25 wagons leaving Belmont. Stationmaster Epsom Downs had to arrange this with the Goods Inspector at Norwood and also advise the Stationmaster at New Cross so that he could arrange for an extra brake van to be sent to Sutton next morning.

In 1911 the maximum load leaving Sutton was reduced to 20 wagons for an E1, but it was often being worked by Radial tanks (usually E4 or E6) which were permitted to take 22 from Sutton to Belmont, 25 beyond and 35 from Banstead to Sutton.

In 1919 the second trip from Belmont ceased as a booked arrangement.

The timing of the Norwood–Epsom Downs trip varied considerably over the years and calls at Waddon or Wallington were inserted or taken out from time to time. From April 1921 the train left Norwood at 9.40 am and ran a trip from Sutton to Hackbridge and back before leaving for Epsom Downs at 12.50 pm.

Fearful of causing delay to the new elelctric trains—shunting at Belmont occupied the running line—the goods was retimed to leave Norwood at 4.20 am from 19th June 1928 arriving at Epsom Downs at 8.45 am whence the engine returned light to Sutton, setting out again light to Belmont at 1.0 pm SO, 1.45 pm SX for trips Belmont to Epsom Downs and back to Norwood calling to shunt Wallington on the way.

From September 1929, however, the train was retimed to leave Sutton at 8.18 am, the times at Belmont and Banstead were reduced and the engine once again returned to Belmont for the outward wagons then back to Epsom Downs and finally to Norwood.

The Southern train crews quickly became accustomed to slick shunting and running between frequent electric trains and these times remained for some time. From 1930 to 1936 the author travelled from Belmont to Sutton on the 8.30 am on his way to school and can testify to the almost unfailing punctuality of the Down morning goods.

From July 1939 the train ceased to go beyond Banstead unless required and the trip back to Belmont had by this time ceased once again.

Also from 1939 the Up train terminated at Sutton. There was no further change until 1947 when the train was again extended to Epsom Downs on a conditional basis and the Up train went through to Norwood except on Saturdays.

The reasons for the decline in railway freight are outside the scope of this story of one branch line. Sufficient to say it became noticeable on the Epsom Downs line in the Summer of 1954 when the daily goods was timetabled to run SX in the Summer and daily during the Winter. From June 1958 the Saturday service ceased altogether. From 1962 to 1966 the train started from Sutton.

From January 1964 the conditional timing to Epsom Downs was withdrawn and in September of that year Banstead Goods Yard was closed, although the train continued to run through to Banstead where there were still two crossovers for run-round purposes.

From June 1965 the train ran on Mondays, Wednesdays and Fridays only and from January 1966 Belmont Goods became a depot for coal only. Freight services on the branch finally ceased with the closure of Belmont Coal depot on 6th January 1969.

The only regular van train ever to operate on the Epsom Downs branch started in 1932. Since electrification of the Victoria to Epsom via Mitcham Junction service in 1929 there had been a 4.28 am vans from Victoria to Sutton. This conveyed news, fish, milk and other parcels and a milk van for Billingshurst which the engine of the 4.28 am (a Battersea E5) attached to the rear of the 5.28 am London Bridge to Brighton via Horsham before returning light, to Eardley for empty coaching stock working.

From a date early in 1932 which the author has not been able to establish—the train first appeared in the July 1932 Working Timetable—the 4.28 am from Victoria was extended to Belmont, thus avoiding the heavy manual transfer at Sutton. After unloading at Belmont station platform the vans were put in the goods yard and picked up later by the daily goods. In 1933 it was extended to Epsom Downs, then in 1934 again terminated at Sutton following introduction of the 6.0 am electric Victoria to Epsom Downs via Mitcham Junction (see Chapter IV).

CHAPTER VI
Race Trains and Other Special Traffic

Spring and Summer meetings have been a feature of the Epsom racing calendar for over 250 years. The Summer meeting, including the "Derby" and "Oaks", was usually during the first week in June. Before World War I and after World War II, there was a second Summer meeting at the beginning of August but although, especially during the nineteenth century, all meetings drew large crowds, in later years the "Derby" became the main attraction.

In the area around Epsom, Derby Week was something of a festival— the highlight of the year. Its approach would be heralded by hordes of gipsies with their horses and caravans converging on the area from all over the country—they made a general nuisance of themselves but it was all part of the scene. On the preceding Sunday—"Derby Sunday"—there would be fairs and jollifications on Epsom Downs and on the railway on this day forests of signals would appear as the Signal Engineer installed the arms on the posts at the three Intermediate signal boxes. Monday would be an anti-climax and Tuesday a warm-up with a number of the less important races taking place watched by relatively small crowds.

The great day would dawn with a feeling of expectancy and on the railway everybody was keyed up and on their toes to perform the mammoth operation of conveying some 80,000 people to Epsom, Epsom Downs and Tattenham Corner.

On the Epsom Downs branch relief signalmen, shunters, porters and ticket collectors would be drafted in from all over the system to supplement the branch staff while locomotive, traffic, Permanent Way and Signal inspectors would be stationed at all key locations. The first train to arrive at Epsom Downs would be the Tool Vans from Battersea to provide rapid assistance in the event of derailment. The locomotive would remain to shunt incoming steam trains. A steam stand-by was provided at Sutton from 8.0 am and in the days of full steam operation there were two shunting pilots provided at Epsom Downs.

The second train to arrive would start from Victoria at 6.30 am picking up at Clapham Junction and Balham and would convey some 600 policemen. In steam days this train was invariably double-headed, as it was a heavy train and was a convenient way of getting one of the shunting pilots to Epsom Downs.

The special train service to Epsom Downs would start around 8.0 am and continue until 2.0 pm; each train in S.R. days carried a Reporting Number. In steam days the branch motor service would be suspended during this period and after A.C. electrification to Sutton these trains would terminate at Wallington between 9.0 am and 1.30 pm.

The special trains would be provided by using spare stock stabled at Eardley Sidings or by making use of suburban and main line trains which were normally stabled at either Eardley or New Cross (Gate) between the morning and evening peaks. Normal passenger trains from London to West Croydon, Wallington, Sutton, Cheam or Epsom Town were also diverted or extended to Epsom Downs and started back from there. Most early special trains were returned empty to London for a second trip and as Epsom Downs could only hold some 15 trains, some of the later ones were also returned empty to various stabling points. In the afternoon the passenger service would be suspended between Banstead and Epsom Downs and empty trains would be queued up buffer to buffer on the Down line under a specially authorised permissive block arrangement.

From the end of Queen Victoria's reign until 1924 an important feature of the day's operating was the passage of the Royal Train, which usually left Victoria about 12.30 pm.

Sutton station on Derby day in those years was seething with noise and excitement as the milling crowds of racegoers built up to a peak and above the noise of the lads selling and shouting "Official Race Cards" would be the thunder of trains, many double-headed, blasting through platform 4 to get some run at the 1 in 60 up to Banstead.

In the days before outside broadcasts the quickest way to find out the name of the winner of the Derby was to go to the local station. Within minutes of the end of the race the result would be passed over the railway omnibus telephone system and at Belmont the signalman would call out the names of the first three to the people gathered on Station Road bridge.

At about 3.30 pm a special fast train would leave for Victoria with press photographers with their pictures for the London evening papers. The problem then facing the railway was that whereas those going to the races had spread themselves over some 5 hours, by about 5.0 pm they all wanted to get home at once, including the Royal family and the occupants of the various first-class and Pullman specials hired by Lord Derby and others. Nearly all this traffic had to be worked across the junction at Sutton in direct conflict with the late afternoon expresses to Portsmouth and returning commuters to Cheam, Epsom and beyond.

Derby Days were not without incident. Dr. Ian C. Allen relates how on one Derby day just after World War I B2x 314 working the 4.53 pm Victoria to Portsmouth Harbour stalled after having been stopped by signal on the gradient approaching Sutton. The Royal Train was about to leave Epsom Downs, but the inspector on duty at Sutton, without a moment's hesitation, organised wrong line order forms and despatched the stand-by locomotove to rescue the failed train which arrived in clear in the Down main platform just seconds before the Royal train appeared slowly round the curve of platform 3 having received an adverse distant signal.

Failures on the rising gradients between Sutton and Banstead were not uncommon; an ex-L.C.D.R. R Class (A658) disgraced herself in this way in 1928 and was assisted by an E4. In 1931 a light aircraft crashed on the line just outside Epsom Downs station at about 5.40 pm. Fortunately no one was seriously hurt and, once the current had been switched off, a gang of men quickly man-handled it clear of the running lines and traffic was resumed after about 25 minutes.

Unlike Tattenham Corner station which received race trains places such as Sheerness, Canterbury, Folkestone, Hastings etc., no long-distance services were run to Epsom Downs; those run from Brighton, Worthing, Portsmouth etc. all ran to Epsom Town.

Apart from race trains the only other special traffic of any significance were the school outings and Sunday School treats to Banstead and Epsom Downs. These were frequently hauled by "Vulcan" 0-6-0's and in Southern days Wainright C Class were fairly frequent visitors, although after 1929 most were electric trains.

During both wars, ambulance and prisoner of war specials appeared on the branch from time to time. At the closing weeks of World War I a surprise arrival at Banstead on an ambulance train was L.&S.W.R. T1 No. 19.

CHAPTER VII
The Decline

As in most places during the Golden Age of railways, the station, stationmaster and his staff were all very much part of the local community. The railway became the lifeline upon which everyone depended for supplies of most of the necessities of life and for transport for all sorts of reasons.

The author remembers the close association Mr. Sawyer, stationmaster at Belmont at the time, kept with his father, the local chemist, and the other shopkeepers in the village in the early 1920's. Porter Albert Gasson came to Belmont in 1920, having started on the L.B.&S.C.R. at Three Bridges. He became involved in the local Boys Brigade and with the local church for which he left the railway in 1938 to become the Verger. Bert, now in his eighties, still lives in Belmont.

The coming of electric trains brought much house building and most people used the railway to get to work, school or for leisure activities. In the 1930's, when the author travelled daily to school in Sutton, it was sometimes not possible to find a seat on the 8.24 am Epsom Downs to London Bridge at Belmont.

The decline started in the 1950's. Personalised transport in the form of motor cars and much improved road systems enabled the bread-winners of Belmont and Banstead to find employment out of London at places such as Dorking, Gatwick Airport, Sevenoaks etc.—all difficult journeys by train. As part of the affluent south east, the area was among the first to see two- and three-car families with the result that off-peak and Sunday travel declined to very low levels. The five-day week killed off most Saturday travel.

Supermarket chains with sophisticated systems of their own for the transport and distribution of their goods and the replacement of house coal and industrial coal by gas, electric or oil-fired central heating disposed of the local goods service.

So, throughout the last 25 years the decline has gone on and the railway is but a shadow of its former self. Gone are the crowds of commuters on the platforms in the morning, gone are the racegoers who now use Tattenham Corner or watch it on TV.

Two trains an hour run almost apologetically up and down the single line between Sutton and Epsom Downs on weekdays only, and one begins to feel that the time cannot be very far away when the Banstead & Epsom Downs Railway will become part of our history.

Bibliography
Epsom Racecourse—Its story and people: D. Hurn
The history of the Derby Stakes: R. Mortimer
A history of Banstead: H.C.M. Lambert
Sutton, Surrey and its surroundings: F. Richards
History of the L.B.&.S.C.R.: J.T. Howard-Turner
A history of the Southern Railway: C.F. Dendy Marshall
The Beacon (Belmont Parish Magazine)
The History of Belmont Hospital: Gareth Edwards
London, Brighton & South Coast Railway working timetables and appendices
Southern Railway Working timetables and appendices

Acknowledgements
Bob Mackmurdie—Divisional Manager, East Croydon B.R.
F.S. Proctor—Chief Civil Engineer, B.R. Southern Region
Dr. Ian C. Allen
Nigel Hearn
Derek Brough

Printed by Bookmag, Henderson Road, Inverness